A Numerology Series

by

Lloyd Leon

FIVE

Life Path Five

Contents

Chapter 1

Understanding Life Path 5

The Significance of Life Path Numbers

The significance of life path numbers lies in their ability to provide insight into an individual's intrinsic traits and potential. For those on Life Path 5, this number symbolizes freedom, adaptability, and a thirst for adventure. Understanding the nuances of life path numbers can empower Life Path 5 individuals to embrace their natural inclinations while also recognizing the areas where growth is essential. By delving into the characteristics associated with Life Path 5, individuals can unlock a deeper understanding of themselves and the unique journey they are on.

Life Path 5 individuals are often characterized by their adventurous spirit and desire for change. This number promotes a sense of curiosity that drives them to explore new experiences and ideas. However, it is vital for Life Path 5s to balance their inherent need for freedom with the responsibilities that come with relationships and commitments. By recognizing the importance of adaptability, they can navigate challenges that arise from their impulsive nature, allowing them to cultivate deeper connections and build meaningful relationships.

Creativity and innovation are essential aspects of Life Path 5, and understanding this significance can lead to personal growth. Life Path 5 individuals are often natural problem solvers, and their creativity can be harnessed in daily life to develop unique solutions to various challenges. By embracing their innovative spirit, they can transform mundane routines into opportunities for exploration and self-expression. This creative outlet not only fosters personal development but also enhances their ability to communicate and connect with others, enriching their relationships.

Travel and adventure are not just hobbies for Life Path 5 individuals; they are vital components of their spiritual and personal growth. Engaging in new experiences allows them to break free from traditional constraints, helping them to cultivate a sense of purpose and direction. These adventures serve as a canvas for self-discovery, offering insights into their values and aspirations. By exploring the world around them, Life Path 5s can integrate spirituality with their journey, allowing for a holistic approach to their personal development.

Ultimately, the significance of life path numbers extends beyond mere categorization; they are tools for self-understanding and growth. For Life Path 5 individuals, embracing their number means acknowledging their strengths while actively working on areas that require attention, such as managing impulsivity and balancing freedom with responsibility. By fostering a supportive community and committing to lifelong learning, they can navigate life's challenges with resilience and grace, ultimately unlocking their true potential and leading fulfilling lives.

Characteristics of a Life Path 5 Individual

Life Path 5 individuals are often characterized by their inherent curiosity and desire for freedom. They thrive on change and are typically drawn to new experiences, which fuels their adventurous spirit. This desire for exploration not only manifests in physical travel but also in a quest for knowledge and personal growth. Life Path 5s are natural learners, constantly seeking to expand their horizons, engage with diverse perspectives, and embrace the unknown. This adaptability allows them to navigate life's unpredictabilities with a sense of ease, making them resilient in the face of challenges.

Creativity and innovation are hallmarks of Life Path 5 individuals. Their open-mindedness often leads them to think outside the box, enabling them to devise unique solutions to problems. This creative energy can be harnessed in various aspects of life, from personal projects to professional endeavors. Life Path 5s are encouraged to cultivate this trait by pursuing artistic interests or engaging in brainstorming sessions that foster collaboration and idea exchange. By embracing their creative potential, they can unlock new pathways for self-expression and fulfillment in both their personal and professional lives.

Despite their adventurous nature, Life Path 5 individuals may struggle with a fear of commitment, particularly in relationships. This fear often stems from their desire for freedom and independence, which can create tension when forming deep connections with others. To build healthy relationships, Life Path 5s must confront this fear and recognize that commitment does not equate to restriction. By fostering open communication and expressing their needs, they can create partnerships that respect their need for autonomy while also nurturing intimacy and trust.

An essential characteristic of Life Path 5 individuals is their ability to communicate effectively. Strong communication skills are integral to their personal growth and success in building connections. They are encouraged to practice active listening and articulate their thoughts clearly to foster understanding in their interactions. This skill not only enhances their relationships but also supports their professional development, as they often find themselves in roles that require negotiation, persuasion, or collaboration. By honing their communication abilities, Life Path 5s can create a more supportive network and contribute meaningfully to their communities.

Finally, Life Path 5 individuals often grapple with balancing their desire for freedom with the responsibilities that come with adulthood. This tension can manifest in career choices, where the allure of flexibility may clash with the need for stability. To navigate this challenge, Life Path 5s must develop strategies for managing impulsivity while remaining focused on their long-term goals. By setting clear intentions and establishing a framework for accountability, they can ensure that their pursuit of freedom does not hinder their growth and success. Embracing both their adventurous spirit and their responsibilities is key to unlocking their true potential and leading a fulfilling life.

Embracing Change as a Core Trait

Embracing change is not merely an external response to life's unpredictability; for individuals on Life Path 5, it is an intrinsic trait that defines their very essence. As Life Path 5 individuals navigate through the world, they are often characterized by their adaptability and readiness to embrace new experiences. This adaptability is not just about reacting to the changes around them; it is about fostering a mindset that welcomes transformation as an opportunity for growth, learning, and self-discovery. Recognizing change as a core trait allows Life Path 5 individuals to harness their unique qualities and turn potential challenges into avenues for exploration.

The essence of change is deeply intertwined with creativity and innovation, two hallmarks of Life Path 5. By embracing change, individuals can unlock their creative potential, allowing them to think outside the box and approach problems with fresh perspectives. This innovative spirit is essential not only in personal endeavors but also in professional settings. Life Path 5 individuals can leverage their ability to adapt to new environments and ideas, inspiring those around them and cultivating an atmosphere of creativity. This dynamic approach to change enhances their capacity to develop solutions that are not only effective but also groundbreaking.

However, the journey of embracing change is not devoid of challenges. Fear of commitment often looms large for Life Path 5 individuals, manifesting as an aversion to settling down or making long-term decisions. This fear can hinder their relationships and personal growth. It is crucial for them to recognize that embracing change does not equate to avoiding commitment; rather, it involves understanding that commitment can evolve. By fostering open communication and a willingness to adapt within relationships, Life Path 5 individuals can build deeper connections that honor both their need for freedom and the bonds they choose to cultivate.

Travel and adventure are integral to the Life Path 5 experience, serving as catalysts for change and self-discovery. The excitement of exploring new places and cultures not only satiates their inherent curiosity but also provides invaluable lessons that contribute to personal growth. Each journey presents an opportunity to embrace change, allowing Life Path 5 individuals to expand their horizons and gain insights into themselves and the world around them. By approaching these adventures with an open mind, they can foster a lifelong learning mindset, enriching their lives and enhancing their adaptability.

Balancing freedom with responsibility is a crucial aspect of navigating change for Life Path 5 individuals. While their desire for independence propels them toward new experiences, it is essential to integrate a sense of responsibility in their pursuits. This balance can be achieved by setting clear intentions and maintaining focus on their goals. By harnessing their natural curiosity and creativity,

Life Path 5 individuals can create a supportive community that encourages growth, accountability, and collaboration. In doing so, they not only embrace change as a core trait but also empower themselves and others to unlock their true potential in a world that is ever-evolving.

Chapter 2

Unlocking Your True Potential

Identifying Personal Strengths

Identifying personal strengths is a crucial step for individuals on the Life Path 5 journey. As those who value freedom, exploration, and adaptability, Life Path 5 individuals often have a unique set of strengths that set them apart. By recognizing these strengths, you can harness them to navigate the changes and challenges life presents. This self-awareness not only fosters personal growth but also enhances your ability to embrace the adventures and opportunities that come your way.

To identify your personal strengths, begin with self-reflection. Consider what activities energize you and bring you joy. For Life Path 5 individuals, this often includes creative pursuits, social interactions, and experiences that involve learning and growth. Take note of situations where you feel most effective or accomplished. This reflection can be enhanced by seeking feedback from trusted friends or mentors who can offer insights into your strengths that you may not readily recognize. Such input can illuminate qualities you possess, such as your adaptability, resourcefulness, and ability to connect with others.

Another effective approach is to engage in assessments designed to reveal your strengths and areas of talent. Tools like personality tests or strength-finding assessments can provide a structured way to uncover your unique attributes. For Life Path 5, these assessments can highlight your capacity for innovation, your curiosity, and your penchant for adventure. Understanding these traits can empower you to seek out experiences that align with your strengths, ultimately leading to a more fulfilling and enriched life.

Embracing change is a natural part of the Life Path 5 experience, and recognizing your strengths can facilitate this process. The ability to adapt and thrive in various circumstances is a hallmark of this path. By identifying your strengths, you create a foundation upon which to build resilience. This resilience allows you to navigate the unknown with confidence, transforming potential obstacles into opportunities for growth. The more you understand what you bring to the table, the better equipped you will be to face challenges head-on.

Ultimately, the journey of identifying personal strengths is ongoing. As you evolve and encounter new experiences, your strengths may also shift and develop. Embrace this fluidity as a hallmark of your Life Path 5 journey. Regularly revisiting your strengths can lead to deeper self-discovery and stronger connections with others. By integrating this understanding into your daily life, you not only foster your own growth but also inspire those around you to embark on their journeys of self-discovery and empowerment.

Setting Goals Aligned with Your Life Path

Setting goals aligned with your life path is crucial for individuals on the Life Path 5 journey. As a Life Path 5, you are naturally inclined toward change, freedom, and exploration. However, without clear goals, your innate desire for adventure can lead to aimlessness. To harness your vibrancy and enthusiasm, it is essential to establish goals that resonate with your core values and life experiences. These goals should not only reflect your passions but also encourage personal growth and provide a sense of direction as you navigate through various transitions.

When setting goals, consider integrating your love for creativity and innovation. Engage in brainstorming sessions where you allow your imagination to roam free. Write down your ideas, no matter how unconventional they may seem. This process can help you identify what truly excites you. For Life Path 5 individuals, goals should be dynamic and adaptable, allowing for shifts as new opportunities arise. Embrace the notion of setting short-term and long-term goals that can evolve, ensuring they remain aligned with your changing interests and circumstances.

Overcoming the fear of commitment is another essential aspect of goal setting for Life Path 5 individuals. By consciously choosing goals that excite you, you can build a greater sense of commitment to your personal and professional aspirations. Focus on goals that foster exploration and growth rather than those that confine you. This can be particularly beneficial in building relationships, as you learn to express your needs and desires while remaining open to the connections that enrich your life. Establishing boundaries within your goals can help create a safe space for commitment without sacrificing your freedom.

Travel and adventure are often integral to the Life Path 5 experience, and these elements can play a significant role in your goal-setting process. Consider setting goals that incorporate travel plans, cultural explorations, or new experiences that enhance your understanding of the world. By aligning your goals with your adventurous spirit, you can create a fulfilling roadmap that allows you to satisfy your curiosity while also achieving personal milestones. This alignment not only nurtures your wanderlust but also fosters a deeper connection with your true self.

In addition to personal exploration, it is vital to balance your goals with responsibility, particularly in your career choices. Aim to set professional goals that allow for freedom while also providing structure. This balance will enable you to pursue your passions without compromising your obligations. Building a supportive community can further enhance your journey, as surrounding yourself with like-minded individuals can provide encouragement and accountability. By integrating these elements into your goal-setting process, you will not only embrace change but also cultivate a life that is rich in experiences, creativity, and meaningful connections.

Overcoming Self-Doubt

Self-doubt can be particularly challenging for individuals on a Life Path 5, who are inherently adventurous and crave freedom. This inner conflict arises when the desire for exploration and change is met with feelings of inadequacy or fear of failure. Overcoming self-doubt requires a conscious effort to reframe negative thoughts and cultivate self-compassion. Recognizing that self-doubt is a common experience, especially for those who thrive in dynamic environments, is the first step toward dismantling its hold. By accepting that self-doubt is not a reflection of one's worth but rather a universal feeling, Life Path 5 individuals can begin to shift their mindset toward empowerment.

One effective strategy for overcoming self-doubt is to embrace the concept of growth mindset. This perspective emphasizes that abilities and intelligence can be developed through dedication and hard work. Life Path 5 individuals can benefit from viewing challenges as opportunities for learning rather than threats to their self-worth. By adopting this mindset, they can approach situations with curiosity and a willingness to experiment, reducing the fear of making mistakes. This shift not only fosters resilience but also enhances creativity, allowing Life Path 5 individuals to explore new ideas and solutions without the paralyzing fear of failure.

Building a supportive community is another crucial aspect of overcoming self-doubt. Life Path 5 individuals often thrive in environments that encourage collaboration and open communication. By surrounding themselves with like-minded individuals who appreciate their adventurous spirit and encourage their growth, they can create a safe space where vulnerability is welcomed. Sharing experiences and challenges with others can diminish feelings of isolation and provide valuable insights. This community can serve as a reminder that everyone experiences self-doubt, reinforcing the idea that it is a normal part of the human experience.

In addition to community support, cultivating strong communication skills is essential to overcoming self-doubt. Life Path 5 individuals can benefit from expressing their thoughts and feelings openly, which not only helps clarify their own emotions but also strengthens their connections with others. Practicing active listening and engaging in meaningful conversations can foster deeper relationships, allowing for mutual support and understanding. As they become more comfortable articulating their experiences, they will find that their self-doubt diminishes, replaced by a sense of confidence and connectedness.

Finally, integrating spirituality and self-discovery into daily practices can be a powerful tool for overcoming self-doubt. Engaging in mindfulness, meditation, or reflective journaling can help Life Path 5 individuals reconnect with their inner selves, allowing them to gain clarity on their values and aspirations. This introspective journey not only enhances self-awareness but also fosters a sense of purpose and direction. By aligning their actions with their true selves, they can navigate the uncertainties of life with greater confidence, ultimately transforming self-doubt into a catalyst for growth and exploration.

Chapter 3

Embracing Change and Adaptability

The Nature of Change for Life Path 5

The journey of a Life Path 5 is inherently intertwined with change, characterized by a dynamic nature that thrives on flexibility and adventure. Individuals on this path often find themselves drawn to a lifestyle rich in variety, constantly seeking new experiences that stimulate their innate curiosity. This ability to embrace change is not merely a trait but a vital aspect of their identity, as it propels them toward personal growth and self-discovery. Understanding this nature of change is essential for Life Path 5 individuals, as it offers insights into how they can unlock their true potential while navigating the complexities of life.

Embracing change requires a mindset that is open to new possibilities and adaptable to shifting circumstances. Life Path 5 individuals often possess a strong desire for freedom, which can sometimes clash with societal expectations or personal commitments. This tension can lead to a fear of commitment, making it crucial for Life Path 5 individuals to explore deeper relationships that allow for both independence and connection. By acknowledging the transformative power of change, they can learn to cultivate relationships that honor their need for freedom while also building meaningful ties with others.

Creativity and innovation are hallmarks of a Life Path 5, and these qualities can be harnessed as tools for navigating change. Engaging in creative pursuits not only allows for self-expression but also serves as a means to adapt to new situations and challenges. Whether through art, writing, or other forms of creativity, Life Path 5 individuals can find solace and inspiration that encourages them to approach change with enthusiasm rather than trepidation. This perspective fosters a habit of lifelong learning, as they become more comfortable with the unknown and more willing to explore uncharted territories.

Exploration and adventure are essential components of the Life Path 5 experience. Travel, in its many forms, offers an invaluable opportunity for self-discovery and personal growth. By stepping outside their comfort zones, Life Path 5 individuals can encounter diverse cultures, perspectives, and ideas that further ignite their curiosity. This journey not only broadens their horizons but also reinforces their ability to adapt to new environments, ultimately enhancing their resilience in the face of change. Such experiences can be profoundly transformative, encouraging a deep connection with the world around them.

To successfully navigate the complexities of change, Life Path 5 individuals must also focus on developing strong communication skills. Effective communication fosters understanding and connection, which are vital for maintaining relationships during times of transition. Additionally, managing impulsivity and enhancing focus are skills that can help mitigate the challenges associated with their adventurous spirit. By integrating mindfulness practices and establishing a supportive community, Life Path 5 individuals can create a stable foundation that balances their desire for freedom with the responsibilities that come with personal and professional commitments. This holistic approach not only empowers them to embrace change but also helps them thrive in their unique life journey.

Strategies for Embracing Change

Embracing change is integral to the journey of a Life Path 5, who thrives on adaptability and exploration. To successfully navigate the ever-shifting landscape of life, it is essential to implement strategies that align with the core characteristics of a Life Path 5. One effective strategy is to cultivate a mindset of flexibility. This involves viewing change not as a disruption but as an opportunity for growth and transformation. By reframing challenges as chances to learn, Life Path 5 individuals can harness the energy of change to foster personal development and uncover new paths.

Another crucial strategy is to engage in continuous learning. Lifelong learning not only satisfies the inherent curiosity of a Life Path 5 but also equips them with the skills and knowledge necessary to adapt to new environments and situations. This can involve pursuing formal education, exploring new hobbies, or engaging in workshops that stimulate creativity. By actively seeking out new experiences, Life Path 5 individuals can keep their minds agile and ready to embrace change, ensuring that they remain resilient in the face of uncertainty.

In addition to learning, building strong communication skills is essential for navigating change effectively. Life Path 5 individuals often find themselves in diverse social settings, and the ability to articulate thoughts, feelings, and ideas clearly is vital. Engaging in active listening and open dialogue fosters deeper connections with others, allowing for the sharing of experiences and insights. This not only enhances personal relationships but also creates a supportive network that can be invaluable during times of transition.

To further support their journey through change, Life Path 5 individuals should prioritize self-discovery and spirituality. Engaging in practices such as meditation, journaling, or reflection can help clarify personal values and goals. Understanding one's purpose and passions provides a solid foundation from which to navigate change with confidence. By integrating spirituality into their daily lives, Life Path 5 individuals can cultivate a sense of inner peace and clarity, allowing them to embrace change as a natural and necessary part of their journey.

Lastly, striking a balance between freedom and responsibility is key for Life Path 5 individuals. While the desire for adventure and exploration is strong, it is important to establish a sense of responsibility in personal and professional commitments. This balance can be achieved by setting clear goals and boundaries that honor both the need for independence and the obligations that come with relationships and career choices. By consciously managing these aspects, Life Path 5 individuals can enjoy the freedom they crave while also fostering stability and growth in their lives.

The Benefits of Adaptability

The concept of adaptability is crucial for individuals on the Life Path 5 journey, as it embodies the essence of growth, transformation, and resilience. Life Path 5 individuals are naturally drawn to change and variety, often thriving in dynamic environments. This inherent flexibility allows them to navigate life's uncertainties with greater ease. By embracing adaptability, Life Path 5s can unlock new opportunities, enhance their creativity, and cultivate a mindset that embraces rather than resists change. This not only fosters personal growth but also enriches their experiences and relationships.

Adaptability encourages a deeper understanding of oneself and the world. Life Path 5 individuals often grapple with the fear of commitment and the desire for freedom, making adaptability essential in balancing these contrasting elements. By learning to adapt, they can explore new relationships and experiences without feeling confined. This flexibility opens doors to diverse experiences, fostering deeper connections with others while enabling them to maintain their individuality. Embracing change becomes an empowering tool, allowing Life Path 5s to navigate their journey with confidence and grace.

Creativity and innovation flourish in environments where adaptability is prioritized. Life Path 5 individuals are often seen as visionaries, and their ability to think outside the box can lead to groundbreaking ideas and solutions. By cultivating adaptability, they can harness their natural curiosity to explore different perspectives and approaches. This not only enhances their creative output but also encourages lifelong learning. Life Path 5s can discover new passions and interests, fueling their desire for self-discovery and growth in both personal and professional realms.

In the context of career choices, adaptability serves as a vital skill for Life Path 5 individuals. The dynamic nature of their interests and aspirations can sometimes lead to impulsivity, making it essential to find a balance between freedom and responsibility. By developing adaptability, they can pivot when necessary, seizing opportunities that align with their evolving goals. This skill allows them to explore various paths without feeling trapped, ultimately leading to a fulfilling career that resonates with their true selves.

Lastly, adaptability plays a crucial role in building supportive communities. Life Path 5 individuals often seek connection and understanding, and their willingness to embrace change fosters an environment where others feel safe to express themselves. By cultivating strong communication skills and an open mindset, they can forge meaningful relationships that thrive on mutual respect and understanding. This supportive network not only enhances personal growth but also reinforces the importance of adaptability as a continuous journey towards unlocking one's true potential.

Chapter 4

Cultivating Creativity and Innovation

The Creative Mind of Life Path 5

The creative mind of a Life Path 5 is a vibrant and dynamic force that thrives on exploration and adaptability. Individuals on this path are often characterized by their innate curiosity and desire for variety, which fuels their creative endeavors. This creativity manifests in numerous ways, from artistic expression to innovative problem-solving. Life Path 5 individuals possess a unique ability to think outside the box, allowing them to approach challenges with fresh perspectives. Embracing this creative aspect is essential for personal growth, as it not only enhances their ability to adapt to change but also fosters a deeper understanding of their true potential.

Central to the creative process for a Life Path 5 is the willingness to embrace change. This adaptability is a double-edged sword; while it allows for the exploration of new ideas and experiences, it can also lead to a fear of commitment.

To harness their creative energy effectively, Life Path 5 individuals must learn to balance their thirst for freedom with a sense of responsibility. This balance enables them to cultivate meaningful relationships and pursue projects that resonate with their core values. By acknowledging the need for stability amidst their adventurous spirit, they can unlock deeper layers of creativity that enhance their life journey.

Travel and adventure are vital components of the Life Path 5 experience, serving as catalysts for creativity. Each new destination offers a wealth of inspiration, exposing individuals to diverse cultures, ideas, and perspectives. This exploration not only broadens their horizons but also ignites their imagination, often leading to innovative solutions in their personal and professional lives. Whether through spontaneous road trips or planned journeys to far-off lands, embracing travel can significantly enrich the creative mind of a Life Path 5, providing invaluable experiences that fuel lifelong learning.

Effective communication plays a crucial role in the development of a Life Path 5's creative potential. By honing their communication skills, these individuals can articulate their ideas clearly and connect with others on a deeper level. This connection fosters collaboration, allowing them to collaborate with like-minded individuals and build a supportive community. Engaging in dialogue about their passions and interests not only enhances their creative output but also strengthens their relationships. As they learn to express themselves more effectively, they become empowered to share their unique perspectives and experiences, further cultivating their creativity.

Finally, integrating spirituality and self-discovery into the creative process can lead to profound personal growth for Life Path 5 individuals. By exploring their inner selves and understanding their motivations, they can channel their creativity in ways that resonate with their authentic selves. Techniques for managing impulsivity and enhancing focus become crucial in this journey, allowing them to maintain a sense of direction while still enjoying the freedom they crave. As they navigate the complexities of their creative minds, the emphasis on spirituality helps them find purpose and fulfillment, ultimately unlocking their true potential as vibrant, innovative beings on the Life Path 5 journey.

Daily Practices to Enhance Creativity

Daily practices play a crucial role in enhancing creativity, especially for individuals on the Life Path 5 journey. Embracing change and adaptability is at the core of Life Path 5, and integrating creativity into daily routines can significantly amplify personal growth. To unlock true potential, it is essential to cultivate an environment that encourages innovative thinking and exploration. Simple practices such as journaling, brainstorming, and engaging in artistic pursuits can help foster a mindset that thrives on creativity and openness.

One effective daily practice is setting aside time for reflection through journaling. This can take the form of free writing, where one writes continuously for a set period without worrying about grammar or structure. This practice allows thoughts to flow freely, uncovering hidden ideas and emotions that can inspire new creative projects.

Additionally, revisiting past entries can provide insights into personal growth and changing perspectives, further enhancing the creative process. For Life Path 5 individuals, who often seek variety, this practice can be a refreshing way to explore different themes and ideas over time.

Engaging in brainstorming sessions can also stimulate creativity. Whether done alone or in collaboration with others, brainstorming encourages the generation of multiple ideas without the pressure of immediate judgment. Setting aside dedicated time each week to explore new concepts, potential projects, or innovative solutions can be incredibly beneficial. Life Path 5 individuals thrive in dynamic environments, and this structured yet flexible approach allows for the exploration of diverse interests while promoting a sense of community and connection with like-minded individuals.

Incorporating artistic practices into daily life can further enhance creativity. This can range from painting and drawing to music and dance, allowing for self-expression in various forms. Experimenting with new mediums or styles can ignite inspiration and break the monotony of routine. For Life Path 5 individuals, who often juggle multiple interests, dedicating time to creative pursuits can serve as a vital outlet for expression and can help manage impulsivity by focusing energy on productive and fulfilling activities.

Lastly, nurturing curiosity is essential for sustaining creativity. Making a habit of exploring new ideas, cultures, and experiences can invigorate the mind and foster innovation. This can be achieved through reading diverse genres, attending workshops, or even traveling to new places. Life Path 5 individuals are naturally inclined towards adventure, and embracing this aspect of their personality can lead to profound insights and creative breakthroughs. By integrating these daily practices, individuals can not only enhance their creativity but also embrace the transformative journey that Life Path 5 embodies.

Fostering Innovation in Everyday Life

Fostering innovation in everyday life is essential for individuals on the Life Path 5 journey, as it aligns with their intrinsic desire for freedom, exploration, and creativity. Life Path 5 individuals often thrive in environments that encourage adaptability and novelty, making it crucial to incorporate innovative thinking into daily routines. By embracing change as a constant companion, Life Path 5 individuals can transform ordinary experiences into opportunities for growth and self-discovery. Simple practices, like rethinking traditional routines or engaging in spontaneous activities, can ignite a spark of creativity and innovation in their lives.

One effective way to foster innovation is through the cultivation of a curious mindset. Life Path 5 individuals possess a natural curiosity that can be harnessed to explore new ideas, perspectives, and experiences. By actively seeking out new knowledge and engaging in lifelong learning, they can enhance their creative capacities and open themselves to fresh insights. Whether it's through reading diverse literature, attending workshops, or simply engaging in meaningful conversations, maintaining a curious approach allows Life Path 5 individuals to continually expand their horizons and innovate in every area of their lives.

Incorporating travel and adventure into daily life can also significantly enhance innovation for Life Path 5 individuals. Travel not only provides a break from routine but also immerses them in diverse cultures and experiences that can stimulate new ideas. By viewing travel as a form of education, Life Path 5 individuals can draw inspiration from the unfamiliar and integrate those lessons into their everyday practices. Planning spontaneous trips or exploring local adventures can rejuvenate their spirit and inspire innovative thinking that transcends traditional boundaries.

Building strong communication skills is another vital aspect of fostering innovation. Life Path 5 individuals often thrive on connection and interaction with others. By honing their ability to communicate effectively, they can share ideas, inspire collaboration, and cultivate relationships that foster creative exchanges. Engaging in active listening and expressing thoughts clearly can lead to fruitful discussions that spark innovative concepts. Moreover, surrounding themselves with a supportive community can amplify their creative energy, as collaborative efforts often yield groundbreaking ideas and solutions.

Lastly, it is important for Life Path 5 individuals to balance their desire for freedom with responsibility. Embracing innovation does not mean neglecting commitments; instead, it involves integrating creativity into obligations. By viewing responsibilities as opportunities for innovation rather than constraints, Life Path 5 individuals can create a harmonious existence that allows for both adventure and accountability. Techniques such as setting clear goals, managing impulsivity, and enhancing focus can facilitate this balance, ensuring that their creative pursuits align with their responsibilities and contribute to their overall growth.

Chapter 5

Overcoming Fear of Commitment

Understanding Commitment Issues

Understanding commitment issues is a crucial aspect for Life Path 5 individuals, who are often characterized by their desire for freedom and adventure. These traits can lead to a natural aversion to commitment, whether in relationships, careers, or personal goals. The challenge lies in navigating this inclination while still fostering meaningful connections and pursuing fulfilling paths. By examining the root causes of commitment issues, Life Path 5s can begin to understand how their need for flexibility can coexist with the stability that commitment offers.

One prominent factor contributing to commitment issues for Life Path 5s is their inherent curiosity and desire for variety. This adventurous spirit can make it difficult to settle into long-term commitments, as the prospect of new experiences often seems more enticing. Understanding this dynamic allows individuals to recognize that their fear of missing out can lead to avoidance behaviors. By reframing their perspective, Life Path 5s can learn to appreciate the depth and richness that committed relationships and endeavors can provide, enhancing their experiences rather than detracting from their freedom.

Moreover, the fear of vulnerability plays a significant role in commitment issues. For many Life Path 5s, the prospect of opening up to another person can be daunting. The desire to maintain independence often clashes with the need for emotional connection. By cultivating strong communication skills and embracing openness, Life Path 5s can create a safe space for both themselves and their partners. This process not only fosters deeper relationships but also allows for personal growth, as individuals learn to balance their need for autonomy with the benefits of intimacy.

Additionally, the journey of self-discovery is essential in addressing commitment issues. Life Path 5s thrive on exploration and change, and this can sometimes lead to a lack of clarity regarding their values and desires. Engaging in practices that promote self-reflection, such as journaling or meditation, can help individuals gain insight into their true motivations. By identifying what commitment means to them and how it aligns with their life path, they can approach relationships and commitments with greater intention and purpose.

Finally, building a supportive community is vital for Life Path 5 individuals seeking to overcome commitment issues. Surrounding themselves with like-minded individuals can provide encouragement and validation as they navigate their fears. This community can serve as a valuable resource, offering diverse perspectives and experiences that highlight the benefits of commitment. By fostering connections with others who understand their journey, Life Path 5s can feel empowered to embrace change while also cultivating strong, lasting relationships that enhance their overall life experience.

Building Healthy Relationships

Building healthy relationships is an essential aspect of personal growth for individuals on Life Path 5. This path is characterized by a deep yearning for freedom, adventure, and exploration, which often translates into a unique approach to relationships. Life Path 5 individuals thrive on variety and excitement, making it crucial to establish connections that honor their need for independence while also fostering genuine emotional bonds. Understanding the dynamics of these relationships can help Life Path 5 individuals unlock their true potential and embrace the changes that come with personal connections.

At the core of healthy relationships is effective communication. Life Path 5 individuals must develop strong communication skills to express their thoughts and feelings openly and honestly. This involves not only sharing their own ideas but also actively listening to their partners. By cultivating a practice of open dialogue, they can create an environment of trust and understanding. This will lead to deeper connections, allowing both partners to feel secure enough to express their needs and desires without fear of judgment or rejection.

Balancing the desire for freedom with the need for commitment can be particularly challenging for Life Path 5 individuals. Often, the fear of losing independence can lead to avoidance of deeper relationships. However, embracing change requires acknowledging that commitment does not equate to confinement. Healthy relationships can provide a supportive space that encourages personal growth and exploration. By redefining commitment as a partnership that allows for individual freedom, Life Path 5 individuals can cultivate relationships that are both fulfilling and liberating.

Moreover, building a supportive community is vital for Life Path 5 individuals. Surrounding themselves with like-minded individuals who understand and appreciate their need for adventure and spontaneity can reinforce their self-discovery journey. Engaging in group activities or exploring new interests together can strengthen these bonds, creating a network of support that encourages growth and creativity. This sense of community not only helps in overcoming feelings of isolation but also nurtures a collective exploration of life's possibilities.

Lastly, embracing change and adaptability in relationships is key for Life Path 5 individuals. As they navigate the complexities of personal connections, it is important to remain open to the evolution of these relationships. People grow and change, and so do their needs and desires. By adopting a mindset of flexibility and openness, Life Path 5 individuals can foster relationships that are resilient and dynamic. This adaptability not only enhances personal connections but also enriches their overall life experience, allowing them to thrive in a world full of possibilities.

Strategies for Emotional Security

Emotional security is a vital aspect of personal growth for those on the Life Path 5 journey. As individuals who thrive on change, adaptability, and exploration, Life Path 5 individuals can sometimes struggle with feelings of instability and uncertainty. To cultivate emotional security, it is essential to develop self-awareness and recognize the triggers that lead to anxiety or fear. Journaling is one effective technique that can help Life Path 5 individuals process their emotions, identify patterns, and articulate their feelings. By regularly reflecting on experiences and emotions, they can create a clearer understanding of their emotional landscape and take proactive steps towards fostering a sense of security.

Building strong relationships is another crucial strategy for enhancing emotional security. Life Path 5 individuals often value their freedom and independence, which can lead to challenges in forming deep connections. However, investing time in nurturing relationships with friends and family can create a solid support system. Engaging in open and honest communication allows individuals to express their needs and boundaries, fostering trust and emotional intimacy. Additionally, participating in group activities or community events can help Life Path 5 individuals connect with like-minded individuals who share their values, thus reinforcing a feeling of belonging.

To further enhance emotional security, Life Path 5 individuals should embrace mindfulness practices. Mindfulness encourages individuals to stay present, reducing anxiety about the future or regrets about the past. Techniques such as meditation or yoga can help cultivate a deeper sense of awareness and acceptance of one's emotions. By learning to observe thoughts and feelings without judgment, Life Path 5 individuals can develop resilience and a greater ability to navigate life's inevitable changes with a sense of calm and balance. This practice not only promotes emotional security but also supports overall mental well-being.

Another effective strategy for emotional security is to harness the power of creativity. Life Path 5 individuals often possess a natural inclination towards creative expression, whether through art, writing, or other forms of innovation. Engaging in creative pursuits can serve as a therapeutic outlet for emotions, allowing individuals to channel their feelings into something tangible. This process can not only enhance emotional clarity but also foster a sense of accomplishment and self-worth. By prioritizing creativity in their daily lives, Life Path 5 individuals can cultivate a stable emotional foundation that supports their adventurous spirit.

Lastly, developing a routine that balances freedom and responsibility is essential for emotional security. While the desire for adventure and spontaneity is strong, establishing a sense of structure can help Life Path 5 individuals feel more grounded. Setting achievable goals and creating a flexible schedule allows for exploration while providing a framework that promotes stability. By incorporating time for self-care, reflection, and personal growth into their routines, Life Path 5 individuals can create a harmonious environment where they feel secure enough to embrace change, pursue their passions, and unlock their true potential.

Chapter 6

Exploring Travel and Adventure

The Wanderlust of Life Path 5

The journey of a Life Path 5 is characterized by an insatiable wanderlust, a desire to explore both the outer world and the depths of the self. This innate curiosity drives Life Path 5 individuals to seek adventure and new experiences, often leading them to diverse cultures, landscapes, and ideas. This wanderlust is not merely about physical travel; it encompasses the exploration of thoughts, philosophies, and creative pursuits. As Life Path 5 individuals embrace change, they discover that each new experience enriches their understanding of the world, allowing them to cultivate a deeper appreciation for the beauty of diversity.

Travel and adventure serve as essential catalysts for growth for Life Path 5 individuals. Each journey taken, whether near or far, provides opportunities for learning and self-discovery. It is through these adventures that they can challenge their perspectives, break free from routine, and ignite their creativity. Life Path 5s often find inspiration in the stories of others, the landscapes they traverse, and the cultures they encounter. This connection to the world around them fosters an innovative mindset, encouraging them to think outside the box and embrace the unknown with open arms.

However, the thrill of exploration can sometimes clash with the need for stability and commitment. Life Path 5s may struggle with the fear of being tied down in relationships or career paths, often leading to impulsive decisions that can hinder their growth. To overcome this fear, it is essential for them to cultivate strong communication skills, allowing them to express their needs and desires effectively. Building authentic relationships based on mutual understanding can provide the support system necessary for Life Path 5 individuals to balance their craving for freedom with the responsibilities of commitment.

As they navigate this balance, Life Path 5s must also learn to harness their curiosity and manage their impulsivity. Techniques such as mindfulness and goal-setting can help enhance focus while still allowing for the spontaneity that defines their nature. By setting intentions for their adventures—whether they are professional endeavors or personal explorations—they can channel their energy into meaningful pursuits. This approach not only fosters personal development but also enriches their lives with experiences that resonate on a deeper level.

Ultimately, the wanderlust of Life Path 5 serves as a powerful metaphor for the journey of self-discovery and personal growth. By embracing change and nurturing their creativity, Life Path 5 individuals can unlock their true potential. Integrating spirituality into their explorations can provide a deeper sense of purpose and connection, guiding them through the complexities of life. As they build a supportive community of like-minded individuals, they can share their experiences, learn from one another, and foster an environment that celebrates both freedom and responsibility. In doing so, Life Path 5s can truly flourish, turning their inherent wanderlust into a transformative force in their lives.

Planning Meaningful Travel Experiences

Planning meaningful travel experiences is essential for individuals on the Life Path 5 journey, as it allows for exploration and self-discovery while embracing change and adaptability. Travel serves as a powerful catalyst for personal growth and transformation, enabling Life Path 5 individuals to step outside their comfort zones and immerse themselves in new environments. When planning your travels, it is crucial to align your itinerary with your core values and interests, ensuring that each experience resonates with your desire for freedom, adventure, and personal development.

To create impactful travel experiences, consider the destinations that ignite your curiosity. Life Path 5 individuals thrive on exploration and learning, so choose places that offer rich cultural experiences, historical significance, or natural beauty. Engage with local communities, participate in workshops, or volunteer for causes that resonate with your spirit. This not only enriches your travel experience but also fosters a sense of connection and purpose, allowing you to cultivate relationships that support your journey of self-discovery.

Another vital aspect of planning meaningful travel experiences is embracing spontaneity while maintaining a flexible itinerary. Life Path 5 individuals often struggle with commitment, making it essential to strike a balance between planning and openness to unexpected opportunities. Allow time within your travel schedule for unplanned adventures, whether it's discovering a hidden gem or joining a local festival. This adaptability not only enhances your travel experience but also strengthens your ability to embrace change in all aspects of life.

Incorporating mindfulness into your travel planning can further deepen your experiences. Take the time to set intentions for your trips and reflect on what you hope to gain from each journey. This practice encourages you to be present and fully engaged in your surroundings, enhancing your ability to learn and grow. Documenting your experiences through journaling or photography can also serve as a powerful tool for reflection and self-discovery, allowing you to track your evolution as you navigate life as a Life Path 5.

Lastly, building a supportive travel community can amplify the impact of your adventures. Connect with fellow travelers or join groups that align with your interests to share experiences and insights. Engaging with like-minded individuals fosters a sense of belonging and encourages collaboration, enriching your journey while providing a network of support. By prioritizing meaningful travel experiences, Life Path 5 individuals can unlock their true potential, embracing the transformative power of exploration and connection in their lives.

Adventure as a Path to Self-Discovery

Adventure serves as a powerful catalyst for self-discovery, particularly for individuals on the Life Path 5 journey. This number symbolizes freedom, adaptability, and exploration, suggesting that embracing new experiences can lead to profound insights about oneself. Adventure, in its many forms—be it travel, artistic pursuits, or simply stepping outside one's comfort zone—allows Life Path 5 individuals to encounter the world with fresh perspectives. Each new experience can illuminate aspects of character that may have remained dormant, fostering personal growth and a deeper understanding of one's true potential.

As Life Path 5 individuals embark on their adventures, they often confront their fears and limitations. This confrontation is essential for development, as it encourages a reevaluation of what one is capable of achieving. By facing challenges head-on, Life Path 5s can dismantle self-imposed barriers, leading to increased confidence and resilience. Every adventure, whether it involves navigating a foreign city or engaging in a spontaneous creative project, becomes an opportunity for growth, pushing boundaries and expanding horizons.

Moreover, adventures can enhance the creativity and innovation that are hallmarks of Life Path 5. Engaging with different cultures, perspectives, and environments stimulates the mind and encourages out-of-the-box thinking. This stimulation is vital for those on this path, as it nurtures their innate curiosity and desire for novelty. Whether through travel or diverse experiences, Life Path 5 individuals can harness these moments to cultivate their imaginative capabilities, allowing them to approach life's challenges with fresh solutions and insights.

Building relationships also becomes more accessible through shared adventures. Life Path 5s often grapple with a fear of commitment, but engaging in adventurous experiences can foster connection and intimacy. When individuals share exciting moments, they create lasting bonds that can transcend superficial interactions. These shared experiences offer a foundation for deeper relationships, encouraging Life Path 5 individuals to embrace vulnerability and develop trust with others, which is crucial for building a supportive community.

Lastly, adventure plays a significant role in the integration of spirituality and self-discovery. For Life Path 5 individuals, exploring the world can lead to reflections on purpose and existence. Nature, travel, and new experiences can serve as conduits for spiritual awakening, prompting profound questions about one's place in the universe. Ultimately, the journey of adventure facilitates a deeper connection with one's inner self, allowing for the harmonization of freedom and responsibility, a crucial balance for those navigating the complexities of Life Path 5. Each adventure undertaken is not merely an external exploration; it is an inward journey that unveils the layers of one's identity, paving the way for a fulfilling and authentic life.

Chapter 7

Developing Strong Communication Skills

The Importance of Effective Communication

Effective communication serves as a cornerstone for personal growth, particularly for individuals on the Life Path 5 journey. This path is marked by a quest for freedom, adventure, and adaptability, all of which thrive in an environment where ideas and emotions can be expressed openly. Life Path 5 individuals are naturally curious and often seek new experiences; however, to fully embrace change and unlock their true potential, they must master the art of communication. This mastery allows for deeper connections with others, fostering relationships that provide both support and inspiration.

In the context of Life Path 5, effective communication is not merely about exchanging information; it is about building rapport and understanding. Life Path 5 individuals often grapple with a fear of commitment or deep connections due to their inherent desire for freedom. By honing their communication skills, they can articulate their needs and boundaries clearly, allowing them to maintain their sense of independence while cultivating meaningful relationships. This balance is essential for personal development, as it enables Life Path 5 individuals to engage with others without compromising their adventurous spirit.

Moreover, effective communication enhances creativity and innovation, which are vital traits for those on this path. Life Path 5 individuals thrive on change and are often drawn to new ideas and projects. When they communicate their thoughts and visions clearly, they invite collaboration and feedback, which can lead to innovative solutions and creative breakthroughs. This exchange of ideas not only enriches their own experiences but also contributes positively to the collective creativity of their communities, encouraging a culture of exploration and growth.

Another significant aspect of effective communication lies in its role in managing impulsivity and enhancing focus. Life Path 5 individuals are known for their spontaneous nature, which can sometimes lead to hasty decisions and scattered energies. By developing strong communication skills, they can engage in reflective dialogues with themselves and others, allowing for mindful consideration of their choices. This practice fosters a greater sense of accountability and responsibility, enabling them to channel their adventurous spirit into productive and fulfilling pursuits.

Ultimately, the journey of a Life Path 5 is intricately linked to the ability to communicate effectively. It opens doors to new adventures, deepens relationships, and allows for the expression of one's true self. By embracing the importance of communication, Life Path 5 individuals can navigate their unique paths with confidence, curiosity, and creativity. As they learn to articulate their ideas and emotions, they not only unlock their own potential but also inspire those around them to embark on their journeys of self-discovery and growth.

Techniques for Enhancing Communication

Effective communication is a cornerstone for personal growth, especially for those on the Life Path 5 journey. As individuals characterized by adaptability, curiosity, and a desire for freedom, Life Path 5s can often find themselves in dynamic situations that require refined communication skills. To enhance communication, one must first cultivate active listening. This technique not only involves hearing the words spoken but also understanding the emotions and intentions behind them. By focusing entirely on the speaker, asking clarifying questions, and reflecting back what is heard, Life Path 5s can create deeper connections and foster a sense of trust in their relationships.

Another vital technique is the practice of assertiveness. Life Path 5 individuals often struggle with impulsivity, which can lead to misunderstandings or conflict. By learning to express thoughts and feelings in a clear, respectful manner, Life Path 5s can advocate for their needs while also considering the perspectives of others. This balance is crucial for maintaining healthy relationships. Assertiveness training, such as role-playing scenarios or employing "I" statements, can help individuals articulate their viewpoints without aggression, thus preventing potential conflicts and promoting mutual respect.

Nonverbal communication plays a significant role in how messages are conveyed and received. Life Path 5s, with their natural affinity for expression, can harness body language, eye contact, and facial expressions to enhance their interactions. Understanding the subtleties of nonverbal cues not only aids in accurately interpreting others' emotions but also allows for a more authentic expression of one's own feelings. Engaging in activities, such as improvisational theater or dance, can help individuals become more aware of their body language and how it impacts communication.

To unlock true potential, embracing the art of storytelling can also be a transformative communication technique for Life Path 5s. Sharing personal experiences and lessons learned creates an emotional connection that can inspire and motivate others. This narrative approach not only captivates audiences but also allows Life Path 5 individuals to reflect on their journey, fostering a deeper understanding of themselves and their values. Practicing storytelling in various formats—be it through writing, public speaking, or even social media—can empower Life Path 5s to share their unique perspectives and insights with the world.

Lastly, incorporating mindfulness into communication can significantly enhance interactions. Life Path 5s often thrive in spontaneous environments, yet this spontaneity can sometimes lead to distractions during conversations. By practicing mindfulness techniques, such as deep breathing or grounding exercises, individuals can improve their focus and presence in discussions. This awareness encourages thoughtful responses rather than impulsive reactions, ultimately leading to more meaningful and productive dialogues. By employing these techniques, Life Path 5s can enrich their communication skills, leading to personal growth and stronger relationships as they navigate their unique life paths.

Building Connections through Dialogue

Building connections through dialogue is a vital aspect of personal growth for individuals on the Life Path 5 journey. As Life Path 5s are naturally curious and adaptable, engaging in meaningful conversations can lead to profound insights and foster relationships that enrich their lives. Dialogue serves not only as a tool for communication but also as a means of exploration, allowing Life Path 5s to articulate their thoughts, fears, and aspirations while receiving feedback that can guide their ongoing journey. Embracing this form of interaction can help them navigate the complexities of change and cultivate deeper connections.

Effective dialogue requires active listening, a skill that Life Path 5s can develop to enhance their interactions. By truly hearing what others have to say, Life Path 5s can foster an environment of trust and openness. This not only aids in building rapport but also encourages a greater exchange of ideas and experiences. Engaging with diverse perspectives can spark creativity and innovation, which are essential for Life Path 5s seeking to express their unique individuality. By remaining open to different viewpoints, they can expand their understanding of the world and their place within it.

Moreover, dialogue provides a platform for Life Path 5s to explore their feelings about commitment and relationships. Many Life Path 5s struggle with the fear of being tied down, leading to challenges in forming lasting bonds. Through open conversations, they can address these fears, articulate their needs, and understand the significance of commitment from a different angle. By sharing their experiences, they not only gain insights into their own behaviors but also learn how to support others in similar situations. This reciprocity strengthens connections and fosters a sense of community.

Travel and adventure are often integral to the Life Path 5 experience, and dialogue can enhance these pursuits. Sharing travel stories or discussing future adventures with like-minded individuals can ignite excitement and inspiration. Conversations about experiences in different cultures or places can broaden perspectives and encourage Life Path 5s to step outside their comfort zones. These dialogues can also lead to opportunities for collaboration, whether through joint travel plans or creative projects inspired by their shared experiences.

Finally, building connections through dialogue aligns with the Life Path 5's quest for lifelong learning. Engaging in discussions not only cultivates strong communication skills but also encourages both personal and collective growth. As Life Path 5s interact with others, they can harness their natural curiosity, seeking knowledge while sharing their insights. This exchange enriches their understanding and helps them balance their desire for freedom with the responsibilities that come with nurturing relationships. Ultimately, embracing dialogue as a fundamental aspect of their journey empowers Life Path 5s to unlock their true potential and create a supportive community that fosters growth and creativity.

Chapter 8

Harnessing Curiosity for Lifelong Learning

The Role of Curiosity in Growth

Curiosity serves as a powerful catalyst for growth, particularly for individuals on the Life Path 5 journey. This life path is characterized by a thirst for adventure, innovation, and a deep-seated desire to explore the world. Curiosity propels Life Path 5 individuals to seek new experiences, challenge established norms, and pursue knowledge in various forms. Embracing curiosity can lead to profound personal growth, enabling individuals to unlock their true potential by broadening their perspectives and expanding their skill sets.

As Life Path 5 individuals navigate change and adaptation, curiosity can help them embrace the unknown rather than fear it. This openness to new ideas and experiences fosters resilience in the face of uncertainty. By cultivating a curious mindset, Life Path 5 individuals can view challenges as opportunities for learning rather than obstacles to their freedom. This shift in perception allows for a more fluid approach to life, where adaptability becomes a strength rather than a source of anxiety.

Moreover, curiosity fuels creativity and innovation, essential traits for Life Path 5 individuals. When curiosity is nurtured, it leads to the exploration of diverse interests and activities, which can spark innovative solutions to problems. Engaging with various disciplines, cultures, and ideas empowers Life Path 5 individuals to think outside the box and approach situations with a fresh perspective. This creative energy not only enhances personal satisfaction but also enriches relationships, as it encourages deeper connections through shared exploration and dialogue.

The interplay between curiosity and commitment is particularly vital for Life Path 5 individuals, who often grapple with a fear of being tied down. By fostering curiosity, they can cultivate a sense of commitment that feels liberating rather than restrictive. This approach encourages them to engage in relationships and commitments that enrich their lives, allowing them to explore the depths of connection without sacrificing their inherent need for freedom. Curiosity can also enhance communication skills, fostering open dialogue and understanding in relationships, which is crucial for building lasting bonds.

In addition to enhancing personal relationships, curiosity plays a significant role in lifelong learning and self-discovery. Life Path 5 individuals are naturally inclined to seek knowledge and experiences that challenge their worldview. By actively engaging with their curiosity, they can pursue various avenues of learning—be it through travel, education, or spiritual exploration. This journey not only leads to personal growth but also aligns with the Life Path 5 ethos of balancing freedom with responsibility. Ultimately, embracing curiosity empowers Life Path 5 individuals to navigate their unique paths with confidence, ensuring that each experience contributes to their ongoing evolution.

Cultivating a Learning Mindset

Cultivating a learning mindset is essential for individuals on the Life Path 5 journey, as it aligns perfectly with their innate curiosity and desire for growth. Life Path 5 individuals thrive in environments that encourage exploration and experimentation. By adopting a learning mindset, they can transform challenges into opportunities for development, fostering resilience in the face of change. Embracing the idea that every experience, whether positive or negative, contributes to personal growth allows Life Path 5 individuals to navigate life's unpredictability with grace and confidence.

One of the core elements of a learning mindset is the willingness to embrace failure as a stepping stone rather than a setback. Life Path 5 individuals often experience a myriad of interests, leading them to try new ventures that may not always succeed. By viewing these experiences as valuable lessons, they can cultivate a sense of resilience and adaptability. This perspective not only enhances their creative problem-solving abilities but also encourages them to take calculated risks, vital for unlocking their true potential.

Curiosity is a powerful driver for lifelong learning, particularly for those on the Life Path 5. Harnessing this natural inclination can lead to exciting discoveries and innovative ideas. Engaging with diverse cultures, exploring new environments, and indulging in various hobbies can significantly broaden their horizons. By actively seeking out new experiences, Life Path 5 individuals can cultivate creativity and innovation, essential traits for both personal and professional growth. This quest for knowledge can also enhance communication skills, as interacting with different perspectives fosters empathy and understanding.

Balancing freedom with responsibility is crucial for Life Path 5 individuals, especially in their pursuit of growth. While the desire for adventure and spontaneity is strong, it is equally important to establish a framework within which this freedom can thrive. Developing techniques for managing impulsivity and enhancing focus can help Life Path 5 individuals channel their energy productively. By setting clear goals and maintaining a commitment to personal development, they can navigate their journeys while still embracing the thrill of exploration.

Lastly, building a supportive community is vital for nurturing a learning mindset among Life Path 5 individuals. Surrounding themselves with like-minded individuals who encourage growth and share similar values can create an environment rich in inspiration. Engaging in discussions, sharing experiences, and collaborating on projects can reinforce their commitment to learning. This support network not only enhances personal growth but also fosters deeper relationships, allowing Life Path 5 individuals to thrive in all aspects of their lives.

Resources for Continuous Learning

To unlock your true potential as a Life Path 5, it is essential to embrace continuous learning as a vital resource. This journey of self-discovery and growth is enriched by various educational tools and platforms that cater specifically to the dynamic nature of Life Path 5 individuals. Online courses, workshops, and webinars provide opportunities for exploration and skill enhancement, allowing you to delve into areas such as personal development, creativity, and adaptability. Websites like Coursera, Udemy, and Skillshare offer an array of topics that align with the curious and innovative spirit of Life Path 5, enabling you to learn at your own pace while connecting with global communities.

Books and literature serve as another invaluable resource for continuous learning. The written word can inspire, educate, and challenge your perspectives, providing insights into the complexities of life and relationships. Seek out authors and thought leaders who resonate with your journey as a Life Path 5. Topics such as overcoming fear of commitment, enhancing communication skills, and cultivating creativity can be deeply explored through the lens of literature. Building a personal library that includes self-help books, biographies, and spiritual texts can foster an environment of growth and reflection, encouraging you to embrace change with an open heart.

Podcasts and audiobooks have emerged as popular mediums for learning, especially for those who thrive on flexibility and convenience. By tuning into podcasts that focus on personal development, adventure, and spirituality, you can immerse yourself in discussions that resonate with your Life Path 5 experiences. Platforms like Spotify and Apple Podcasts offer a diverse range of content that can help you navigate challenges such as impulsivity and the balance between freedom and responsibility. Listening to experts share their knowledge and experiences can spark new ideas and motivate you to apply what you learn in your daily life.

Engaging with a community of like-minded individuals can enhance your learning experience significantly. Joining online forums, local meetups, or social media groups dedicated to Life Path 5 and numerology can provide a supportive network where you can share insights, ask questions, and celebrate each other's growth. Collaborative learning environments encourage creativity, as you engage in discussions and exchange ideas that can lead to innovative solutions and approaches in your personal and professional life. Building relationships within this community can also help you overcome fears and strengthen your communication skills, paving the way for deeper connections and shared experiences.

Finally, integrating mindfulness and self-reflection into your learning journey is crucial for Life Path 5 individuals. Techniques such as journaling, meditation, and mindfulness practices can help you process what you learn, recognize your progress, and maintain focus amidst distractions. By taking the time to reflect on your experiences and insights, you cultivate a deeper understanding of yourself and your path. This commitment to personal growth not only enhances your adaptability and creativity but also prepares you to navigate the ever-changing landscape of life with resilience and confidence. Embracing continuous learning ensures that you remain open to new experiences, fostering a life rich with adventure and fulfillment.

Chapter 9

Balancing Freedom and Responsibility

The Dual Nature of Life Path 5

The dual nature of Life Path 5 embodies a complex interplay between freedom and responsibility, adventure and stability, creativity and focus. Those navigating this life path often find themselves torn between the desire for exploration and the need to establish roots. This duality can create a rich tapestry of experiences that fosters personal growth and innovation, yet it can also lead to internal conflict and uncertainty. Understanding this inherent tension is crucial for Life Path 5 individuals as they seek to unlock their true potential and embrace the changes that life presents.

On one hand, Life Path 5 is characterized by a thirst for adventure and an insatiable curiosity. Individuals on this path are often drawn to new experiences, travel, and the thrill of the unknown. This adventurous spirit fuels their creativity and innovation, allowing them to see the world from unique perspectives. However, this need for freedom can sometimes give rise to a fear of commitment, making it difficult to form stable relationships or pursue long-term goals. Acknowledging and embracing this duality enables Life Path 5 individuals to balance their desire for exploration with the importance of grounding themselves in meaningful connections and responsibilities.

Conversely, the other side of the Life Path 5 experience is the challenge of navigating responsibilities and the fear that accompanies commitment. As they grapple with the inevitability of change, those on this path may struggle with impulsivity and distraction. Learning to manage these tendencies is vital for personal growth. Techniques that enhance focus and promote self-discipline can help Life Path 5 individuals channel their abundant energy into productive avenues. By developing strong communication skills and building a supportive community, they can foster relationships that provide stability while still allowing for the freedom they crave.

Furthermore, the dual nature of Life Path 5 encourages a deep exploration of spirituality and self-discovery. This journey often involves embracing the unknown and seeking deeper truths about oneself and the universe. Through practices such as meditation, journaling, or engaging in creative expression, Life Path 5 individuals can cultivate a greater sense of self-awareness. This heightened understanding can serve as a guiding compass, helping them navigate the complexities of their dual nature while also enhancing their capacity for adaptability.

Ultimately, embracing the dual nature of Life Path 5 is about finding harmony between freedom and responsibility, adventure and stability. By recognizing and accepting these contrasting impulses, individuals can unlock their true potential. Through intentional practices that foster creativity, effective communication, and a strong community, Life Path 5 individuals can turn their inherent challenges into powerful catalysts for growth. It is this journey of embracing change that allows them to thrive, not just in their personal lives, but in their broader contributions to the world around them.

Making Conscious Career Choices

Making conscious career choices is essential for individuals on the Life Path 5 journey, as it allows them to align their professional lives with their intrinsic values and passions. Life Path 5 individuals are known for their adaptability and desire for freedom, which can lead to a unique set of challenges when it comes to selecting a career. The key lies in understanding that every choice contributes to their growth and self-discovery. By engaging in conscious decision-making, Life Path 5s can navigate their careers in a way that honors their need for variety while also fostering stability and fulfillment.

Embracing change and adaptability is a hallmark of Life Path 5, and these qualities can be harnessed to explore diverse career options. Rather than feeling confined to a single path, individuals can view their career as a journey filled with opportunities for exploration and learning. This perspective encourages them to seek out roles that not only challenge their skills but also ignite their curiosity. By consciously considering how each potential career aligns with their desire for novelty and growth, Life Path 5s can make informed choices that lead to satisfying professional lives.

Cultivating creativity and innovation is another vital aspect of making conscious career choices. Life Path 5s thrive in environments that encourage imaginative thinking and allow for self-expression. When evaluating career options, individuals should look for roles that provide the freedom to innovate and contribute unique ideas. This can involve seeking positions in dynamic industries, such as technology, arts, or entrepreneurship, where their creativity can flourish. By prioritizing roles that align with their creative instincts, Life Path 5s can enhance their sense of purpose and satisfaction in their work.

Overcoming the fear of commitment is crucial for Life Path 5 individuals as they navigate their career paths. The desire for freedom might lead to hesitation in settling into a long-term role or commitment. However, conscious career choices can help them frame commitment as a positive aspect of their professional journey. By recognizing that commitment does not equate to confinement, Life Path 5s can build relationships within their chosen fields that offer support and growth. This understanding can lead to meaningful collaborations and opportunities that resonate with their values.

Finally, integrating spirituality and self-discovery into the career decision-making process can profoundly impact Life Path 5 individuals. By taking the time to reflect on their spiritual beliefs and personal values, they can gain clarity about what they truly want from their careers. This introspective approach allows them to make decisions that not only fulfill their professional ambitions but also align with their inner selves. By cultivating a supportive community of like-minded individuals, Life Path 5s can share experiences and insights, reinforcing their commitment to making conscious choices that propel them toward their true potential.

Integrating Freedom into Professional Life

Integrating freedom into professional life is essential for individuals on the Life Path 5 journey, as it aligns with their innate desire for exploration, innovation, and adaptability. A career that embraces this need for freedom allows Life Path 5 individuals to thrive, enabling them to express their creativity and pursue their passions without feeling confined by rigid structures. In a world where traditional career paths often emphasize stability and predictability, Life Path 5 individuals can redefine success by integrating flexibility into their professional choices, allowing them to remain true to their authentic selves.

To effectively integrate freedom into professional life, Life Path 5 individuals should seek out roles that encourage autonomy and creativity. This might mean pursuing freelance opportunities, entrepreneurship, or positions within organizations that foster a culture of innovation. By prioritizing environments that value flexibility, these individuals can align their work with their core values, which include curiosity and adaptability. Finding a job that allows for self-expression not only enhances job satisfaction but also cultivates a sense of purpose, making it easier to navigate the inevitable changes that come with professional life.

One of the challenges Life Path 5 individuals may face is the fear of commitment, which can affect their professional relationships and stability. Overcoming this fear requires a mindset shift that embraces the idea that commitment does not equate to confinement. Establishing clear boundaries and maintaining open communication can help Life Path 5 individuals build strong professional relationships while still enjoying a sense of freedom. By viewing commitment as a choice rather than a restriction, they can foster collaboration and teamwork without sacrificing their independence.

Another crucial aspect of integrating freedom into professional life is balancing personal interests with responsibilities. Life Path 5 individuals are known for their diverse interests and passions, which can sometimes lead to impulsivity or difficulty in focusing on one particular goal. Developing techniques to manage this impulsivity can help in channeling their energy toward productive outcomes. This might include setting specific goals, creating structured routines, or engaging in mindfulness practices that enhance concentration. By mastering focus, Life Path 5 individuals can harness their creativity and curiosity to achieve their professional aspirations while maintaining their freedom.

Finally, building a supportive community is vital for Life Path 5 individuals as they navigate their unique professional journeys. Surrounding themselves with like-minded individuals who understand their desire for freedom and exploration can provide encouragement and inspiration. Networking with other Life Path 5s or individuals who share similar values can lead to collaborative opportunities and shared experiences. This sense of community fosters an environment where creativity and adaptability are celebrated, reinforcing the importance of integrating freedom into their professional lives while contributing to personal growth and fulfillment.

Chapter 10

Integrating Spirituality and Self-Discovery

Exploring Spirituality as a Life Path 5

Exploring spirituality as a life path 5 involves recognizing the dynamic interplay between personal freedom and the quest for deeper understanding. Life path 5 individuals are naturally drawn to experiences that challenge the status quo and ignite their curiosity. This journey often leads to exploring various spiritual philosophies and practices that resonate with their need for adaptability and growth. Spirituality, in this context, becomes a vehicle for self-discovery, enabling life path 5s to connect with their inner selves and the broader universe in meaningful ways.

As life path 5s embrace change, spirituality offers a framework for navigating life's uncertainties. This flexibility allows them to engage with diverse spiritual traditions, integrating elements that align with their unique perspectives. Whether through meditation, mindfulness, or engaging with nature, these practices can enhance their ability to remain grounded while exploring the ever-changing landscape of their lives. The spiritual journey encourages life path 5s to cultivate resilience and develop coping strategies that support their adventurous spirit.

Creativity and innovation play a pivotal role in the spiritual exploration of life path 5 individuals. By tapping into their imaginative faculties, they can express their spiritual insights through art, writing, or other creative outlets. This process not only fosters personal growth but also encourages the expansion of their spiritual understanding. Engaging in creative practices allows life path 5s to articulate their experiences and beliefs, ultimately leading to a more profound connection with themselves and the world around them.

Furthermore, the theme of commitment and relationships is intricately woven into the spiritual journey for life path 5s. Their natural inclination towards freedom can sometimes lead to a fear of commitment, yet spirituality invites them to explore the deeper connections they can forge with others. By embracing vulnerability and authenticity in their relationships, life path 5s can cultivate a supportive network that encourages their spiritual growth. This support system is essential as they navigate the complexities of their personal and spiritual lives.

Ultimately, integrating spirituality into the life path 5 journey involves a continuous process of self-discovery and learning. As they harness their curiosity, life path 5s can approach spirituality with an open heart and mind, allowing for an enriching exploration of their beliefs and experiences. This journey not only enhances their capacity for personal growth but also aligns with their intrinsic desire for adventure and profound understanding. By embracing spirituality, life path 5 individuals can unlock their true potential, leading to a fulfilling and balanced life that honors both their need for freedom and their quest for deeper meaning.

Practices for Self-Discovery

Self-discovery is a vital journey for individuals on Life Path 5, as it directly influences their ability to embrace change and unlock their true potential. This process begins with introspection, where individuals take the time to explore their thoughts, feelings, and motivations. Journaling is a powerful tool in this regard; by writing regularly, Life Path 5 individuals can articulate their experiences, desires, and fears. This practice not only promotes self-awareness but also helps in identifying patterns that may hinder growth or reinforce limiting beliefs. By reflecting on their entries, they can gain insights into their reactions to change and develop a deeper understanding of their unique path.

Another effective practice for self-discovery is engaging in varied experiences that challenge the status quo. Life Path 5s thrive on adventure and exploration, making it essential to step outside their comfort zones. Traveling, whether to distant lands or local hidden gems, allows them to encounter new perspectives and cultures, fostering adaptability and resilience. Each new experience serves as a mirror reflecting their strengths and weaknesses, encouraging them to embrace their innate curiosity. This exploration not only enriches their lives but also enhances their ability to connect with others, a critical component in building meaningful relationships.

Mindfulness and meditation are also significant practices for Life Path 5 individuals seeking self-discovery. These techniques help cultivate a sense of presence and awareness, enabling them to sift through their thoughts without judgment. By creating a quiet space for reflection, they can better understand their impulses and desires, which are often heightened in this life path. Regular mindfulness practice promotes emotional regulation, allowing individuals to respond to life's uncertainties with composure rather than reactive tendencies. Ultimately, this leads to a more profound connection with their inner selves and the ability to navigate challenges with grace.

Developing strong communication skills is crucial for Life Path 5 individuals as they journey through self-discovery. Engaging in open dialogues with trusted friends or mentors can provide valuable feedback and support. These conversations often reveal blind spots and can challenge preconceived notions, pushing individuals toward growth. Additionally, participating in workshops or groups focused on personal development can enhance their ability to articulate thoughts and feelings. This improvement in communication not only strengthens their relationships but also fosters a sense of community, which is essential for their growth and fulfillment.

Finally, integrating spirituality into the self-discovery process can be transformative for Life Path 5s. Spiritual practices such as yoga, prayer, or connecting with nature can provide a deeper sense of purpose and belonging. These practices encourage individuals to explore their beliefs about life and existence, facilitating a stronger connection to their true selves. By aligning their actions with their spiritual values, they can navigate the complexities of life with clarity and purpose. Embracing spirituality as a tool for self-discovery allows Life Path 5 individuals to maintain balance in their quest for freedom while fulfilling their responsibilities, ultimately leading to a more authentic and enriched life experience.

Aligning Spirituality with Daily Life

Aligning spirituality with daily life is a transformative journey for individuals on a Life Path 5. It requires an understanding of how spiritual beliefs and practices can seamlessly integrate into the fabric of everyday experiences. For those who resonate with the traits of a Life Path 5—adaptability, curiosity, and a thirst for adventure—embracing spirituality can provide a grounding force. It encourages a deeper connection to oneself and the world, fostering a sense of purpose amidst the unpredictability that often characterizes this path.

To begin this alignment, it is essential to establish a daily spiritual practice that resonates with personal values and beliefs. This could be as simple as morning meditation, journaling reflections, or engaging in mindful breathing exercises throughout the day. Such practices create a space for self-reflection and help to cultivate awareness of one's thoughts and feelings. For Life Path 5 individuals, who often thrive on spontaneity, incorporating small rituals can serve as anchors, allowing them to navigate their dynamic lives with greater ease and clarity.

Another key aspect of aligning spirituality with daily life is the cultivation of creativity and innovation. Life Path 5 individuals are naturally creative and inclined toward new experiences. By viewing creativity as a spiritual practice, one can unlock deeper insights and inspiration. Engaging in creative activities—be it through art, writing, or even problem-solving—can become a form of spiritual expression. This not only enhances personal growth but also fosters a sense of community when shared with others, reinforcing connections that are vital for Life Path 5 individuals who often seek meaningful relationships.

In addition to creativity, embracing travel and adventure as spiritual experiences can profoundly enrich daily life. Life Path 5 individuals are drawn to exploration, and when approached with a spiritual mindset, each journey becomes an opportunity for self-discovery. Whether traveling to new countries or exploring local environments, the experiences gained can provide valuable lessons and insights. Keeping a travel journal to document thoughts and emotions during these adventures can further enhance spiritual alignment, making each trip a profound learning experience.

Finally, balancing freedom with responsibility is an essential component of integrating spirituality into daily life. Life Path 5 individuals often grapple with a fear of commitment, which can hinder personal and spiritual growth. By recognizing that commitment to one's spiritual journey does not equate to a loss of freedom, a healthier perspective can emerge. This balance enables individuals to build strong relationships and communities that support their growth while allowing for the exploration and freedom they cherish. By embracing and aligning spirituality with daily routines, Life Path 5 individuals can unlock their true potential, fostering a life rich in purpose, creativity, and connection.

Chapter 11

Managing Impulsivity and Enhancing Focus

Recognizing Impulsive Behaviors

Recognizing impulsive behaviors is an essential step for individuals on the Life Path 5 journey. Life Path 5s are often characterized by their adventurous spirit, boundless curiosity, and a strong desire for freedom. However, this innate yearning can sometimes lead to impulsive actions that disrupt personal growth and hinder the development of meaningful relationships. Understanding these behaviors involves self-awareness and a willingness to reflect on one's actions and motivations. By recognizing impulsivity, Life Path 5s can cultivate a more balanced approach to their adventurous nature.

Impulsivity often manifests in various forms, including spontaneous decisions that may overlook long-term consequences. For example, a Life Path 5 might decide to embark on an unplanned trip without considering financial obligations or personal commitments. While spontaneity can lead to exciting experiences, it is crucial to evaluate the impact of such decisions on overall life balance. By acknowledging these moments of impulsivity, individuals can learn to pause and assess their motivations, leading to more thoughtful choices that align with their true potential.

Another aspect of impulsive behavior is the tendency to seek immediate gratification. Life Path 5s may find themselves jumping from one interest to another, pursuing fleeting passions rather than allowing themselves the time to cultivate deeper skills or relationships. This pattern can result in a lack of fulfillment and a sense of restlessness. Recognizing this tendency is vital in cultivating creativity and innovation; by understanding the difference between healthy exploration and impulsive diversions, Life Path 5s can focus their energy on endeavors that resonate with their core values and long-term goals.

Furthermore, impulsivity can create challenges in building and maintaining relationships. Life Path 5 individuals often crave freedom, which may lead them to avoid commitment or act without considering the feelings of others. Recognizing when impulsive behaviors disrupt relationship dynamics is essential for fostering deeper connections. Engaging in open communication and being mindful of how impulsive actions affect loved ones can help Life Path 5s develop healthier, more supportive relationships that honor both their desire for adventure and the needs of others.

Finally, managing impulsivity is a continual process that requires practice and self-discipline. Techniques such as mindfulness, setting clear goals, and establishing accountability can enhance focus and reduce impulsive tendencies. By integrating these practices into daily life, Life Path 5s can embrace their unique journey while maintaining a balanced approach to freedom and responsibility. This recognition and management of impulsive behaviors ultimately pave the way for a more fulfilling life, rich in creativity, meaningful connections, and personal growth.

Techniques for Improved Focus

Improving focus is essential for individuals on the Life Path 5 journey, as it allows for the harnessing of one's innate creativity and adaptability. Life Path 5 individuals often thrive in environments filled with change and spontaneity, but without effective focus, these qualities can lead to distraction and scattered energy. Cultivating techniques to enhance concentration can empower Life Path 5 individuals to channel their diverse interests into meaningful pursuits. This chapter will explore practical strategies that can facilitate improved focus, enabling Life Path 5 individuals to fully embrace their potential.

One effective technique for improving focus is the practice of mindfulness meditation. This practice encourages individuals to engage in the present moment, fostering a deeper awareness of thoughts and feelings as they arise. For a Life Path 5 individual, who may naturally gravitate towards a multitude of experiences, mindfulness can serve as an anchor. Regular meditation can help in quieting the mind, reducing anxiety, and clearing mental clutter, thereby allowing for enhanced concentration on the tasks at hand. By dedicating a few minutes each day to mindfulness practice, Life Path 5 individuals can cultivate a greater sense of clarity and purpose in their daily activities.

Another important technique is the establishment of a structured routine that accommodates flexibility. Life Path 5 individuals often resist rigid schedules due to their desire for freedom and variety. However, creating a loose structure can provide the necessary framework to enhance focus without stifling creativity. By designating specific times for work, creative pursuits, and leisure, individuals can ensure that they allocate time for their passions while still maintaining a sense of order. This balance allows for the cultivation of focus during dedicated work periods while leaving room for spontaneous exploration and adventure.

Setting achievable goals with clear intentions can also significantly enhance focus for Life Path 5 individuals. By breaking larger projects into smaller, manageable tasks, individuals can maintain a sense of progress and accomplishment. This approach not only helps in mitigating feelings of overwhelm but also reinforces motivation. Utilizing tools such as vision boards or journals can assist in visualizing these goals, providing ongoing inspiration and reminders of what one hopes to achieve. As Life Path 5 individuals witness their progress, they can build confidence in their ability to maintain focus and reach their aspirations.

Lastly, surrounding oneself with a supportive community can play a pivotal role in enhancing focus. Engaging with like-minded individuals who understand the unique challenges and strengths of Life Path 5 can create an environment that fosters accountability and encouragement.

By sharing experiences, insights, and strategies, members of this community can motivate one another to stay committed to their goals. This collective energy can amplify individual efforts, transforming the experience of maintaining focus into a shared journey of growth and discovery.

Incorporating these techniques into daily life can empower Life Path 5 individuals to cultivate improved focus and channel their diverse talents effectively. By practicing mindfulness, establishing flexible routines, setting achievable goals, and fostering supportive relationships, individuals can navigate their path with greater clarity and purpose. Embracing these strategies will not only enhance focus but will also enrich the overall experience of living authentically as a Life Path 5, unlocking their true potential in the process.

Creating a Balanced Routine

Creating a balanced routine is essential for individuals on the Life Path 5 journey, as it allows them to harness their natural tendencies toward freedom and adaptability while ensuring they do not lose sight of their goals and responsibilities. Life Path 5 individuals are often characterized by their adventurous spirits, curiosity, and desire for continuous growth. However, without a balanced routine, these traits can lead to impulsivity and scattered energies, making it challenging to achieve their true potential. Establishing a daily structure that accommodates spontaneity while incorporating essential tasks can help Life Path 5s maintain their motivation and focus.

To begin crafting a balanced routine, it is crucial for Life Path 5s to identify their core values and priorities. This process involves self-reflection and honest assessment of what truly matters to them. By determining their most important goals, whether they relate to personal growth, relationships, or career aspirations, individuals can begin to allocate their time and energy more effectively. Creating a vision board or a written manifesto can serve as a constant reminder of these priorities, helping to steer daily choices and commitments toward fulfilling their true potential.

Incorporating flexibility into a routine is vital for the naturally dynamic Life Path 5. While consistency offers a framework for productivity, it is equally important to leave room for exploration and spontaneity. Life Path 5 individuals thrive on new experiences, and a rigid schedule may feel stifling. To achieve this balance, consider setting aside specific time slots for both structured activities and unplanned adventures. This approach not only fosters creativity but also allows for the spontaneous moments that recharge their spirits, making the routine feel less like a chore and more like a dynamic journey.

Another vital aspect of creating a balanced routine is establishing healthy boundaries in relationships and personal commitments. Life Path 5s often grapple with a fear of commitment, which can lead to overextending themselves in various areas of life. To combat this, it's essential to learn to say no to obligations that do not align with their core values or that may hinder their growth. Open communication with loved ones about needs and boundaries can help foster understanding and support, allowing Life Path 5 individuals to maintain their freedom while nurturing meaningful connections.

Lastly, integrating practices that promote self-awareness and mindfulness into the daily routine can significantly enhance focus and manage impulsivity. Techniques such as meditation, journaling, or even creative activities like painting or music can ground Life Path 5s, helping them to cultivate patience and clarity. These practices not only improve concentration but also serve as tools for self-discovery and spiritual growth. By embracing a balanced routine infused with creativity, flexibility, and self-reflection, Life Path 5 individuals can navigate their unique paths with confidence, transforming their lives into a rich tapestry of adventure and achievement.

Chapter 12

Building a Supportive Community

The Importance of Community for Life Path 5

The importance of community for individuals on Life Path 5 cannot be overstated, as it serves as a crucial support system that nurtures their inherent need for freedom and exploration. Life Path 5 individuals thrive in environments that encourage adaptability and creativity, and a strong community can provide the necessary framework for these traits to flourish. Being surrounded by like-minded individuals fosters a sense of belonging and acceptance, which can alleviate the feelings of restlessness that often accompany this life path. Engaging with a supportive network allows Life Path 5 individuals to share their experiences, insights, and aspirations, ultimately enhancing their personal growth and self-discovery.

Building relationships within a community can also help Life Path 5 individuals overcome their fear of commitment. The dynamic nature of their personality often makes them hesitant to engage deeply with others, fearing that such connections may limit their freedom. However, a nurturing community can demonstrate that commitment does not equate to confinement. Instead, it can provide a safe space for exploration and expression, where members encourage each other to pursue their passions while maintaining their autonomy. This understanding can help Life Path 5 individuals develop healthier relationships, fostering a sense of trust and stability that complements their adventurous spirit.

In addition to emotional support, community engagement can significantly enhance creativity and innovation in daily life. Life Path 5 individuals possess a natural curiosity and zest for new experiences, which can be amplified through collaborative efforts. Participating in group activities, workshops, or creative endeavors allows them to exchange ideas and gain fresh perspectives. This interaction not only stimulates their imagination but also encourages them to step outside their comfort zones, leading to personal and artistic growth. By cultivating a vibrant community, Life Path 5 individuals can harness the collective energy and creativity of their peers, resulting in innovative solutions and new avenues for self-expression.

Moreover, a supportive community can play a pivotal role in managing the impulsivity that often accompanies Life Path 5. The desire for constant change and new experiences can sometimes lead to hasty decisions and a lack of focus. By surrounding themselves with individuals who understand their journey, Life Path 5s can gain valuable insights and guidance. These connections provide opportunities for accountability and reflection, helping them to develop strategies for channeling their energy more effectively. A strong community encourages open communication, allowing Life Path 5 individuals to articulate their goals and challenges while receiving constructive feedback that promotes personal development.

Finally, the integration of spirituality and self-discovery within a community setting can profoundly impact Life Path 5 individuals. Engaging with others who share similar spiritual interests or practices can facilitate deeper exploration of their inner selves. This shared journey fosters a sense of connection and understanding, allowing them to navigate their personal paths with greater clarity and confidence. By participating in community-based spiritual activities, Life Path 5 individuals can embrace change and adaptability while grounding themselves in their values and beliefs. This synergy between community and spirituality ultimately empowers Life Path 5 individuals to unlock their true potential and live authentically in alignment with their life purpose.

Finding Like-Minded Individuals

Finding like-minded individuals is a crucial step for those on the Life Path 5 journey, as it provides a supportive environment that nurtures creativity and adaptability. Life Path 5 individuals thrive on change, adventure, and exploration, making connections with others who share similar values essential. By surrounding themselves with like-minded people, Life Path 5s can engage in meaningful conversations, share experiences, and inspire one another to overcome challenges. This community can serve as a catalyst for personal growth, encouraging each individual to embrace their unique qualities while fostering a sense of belonging.

One effective way to find like-minded individuals is by participating in groups or activities that resonate with your interests and passions. Whether it's joining a travel club, attending workshops focused on creativity, or engaging in discussions about spirituality, these spaces offer opportunities to meet others who align with your aspirations. Online platforms can also be beneficial, as they provide access to global communities where Life Path 5s can connect with others who share their thirst for knowledge and adventure. Engaging with these communities can lead to collaborative projects, friendships, and a deeper understanding of oneself.

Networking events and local meetups can be particularly advantageous for Life Path 5 individuals who are looking to build relationships grounded in shared values. These gatherings often attract individuals who are open-minded and eager to explore new ideas, making them ideal settings for meaningful interactions. By actively participating in discussions and expressing your thoughts, you can attract others who resonate with your perspectives. This not only enhances your communication skills but also cultivates the confidence needed to navigate social situations, which can sometimes be a challenge for Life Path 5s.

Moreover, volunteering for causes that inspire you can be another excellent way to meet like-minded individuals. Engaging in service-oriented activities not only allows you to contribute positively to the community but also connects you with others who are driven by similar motivations. These interactions often lead to deeper conversations and friendships forged through shared experiences. Such environments foster collaboration and innovation, which are essential for Life Path 5s seeking to harness their creativity and adaptability.

Lastly, embracing the idea of lifelong learning can also facilitate connections with like-minded individuals. Participating in classes, workshops, or seminars allows Life Path 5s to meet others who share a commitment to personal growth and exploration. By immersing yourself in an environment that values curiosity, you can discover new perspectives and ideas that enrich your journey. In turn, these connections can help build a supportive community that encourages you to navigate the complexities of life while remaining true to your free-spirited nature.

Nurturing Relationships within the Community

Nurturing relationships within the community is essential for individuals on the Life Path 5 journey. As Life Path 5s are known for their adventurous spirits and love of freedom, they often thrive in environments that foster connection and collaboration. Building a supportive network not only enhances personal growth but also encourages the sharing of ideas and experiences that can lead to greater creativity and innovation. By actively engaging with others, Life Path 5s can cultivate relationships that inspire them to embrace change, explore new opportunities, and express their unique talents.

To nurture relationships effectively, Life Path 5 individuals must first embrace their natural curiosity. This trait allows them to connect deeply with others by showing genuine interest in their stories and perspectives. Engaging in conversations that explore shared interests, values, and goals can lead to meaningful connections. Additionally, participating in community events or workshops can provide a platform for Life Path 5s to meet like-minded individuals who share their passion for adventure and personal growth. These interactions can result in lasting friendships that support their journey toward unlocking true potential.

Communication is a vital component of nurturing relationships, and Life Path 5s can enhance their skills in this area through active listening and open dialogue. By being present in conversations and valuing the input of others, they can foster an atmosphere of trust and respect. This not only builds stronger connections but also encourages collaboration and the exchange of ideas. Life Path 5s can benefit from practicing empathy, which will enable them to understand and appreciate the diverse perspectives within their community, ultimately enriching their own experiences.

Overcoming the fear of commitment is another crucial aspect of building relationships for Life Path 5s. While their desire for freedom may create apprehension towards long-term commitments, it is essential to recognize that deep connections often require a level of vulnerability and dedication. By reframing commitment as a choice that enhances their adventurous spirit rather than constraining it,

Life Path 5s can engage more meaningfully with others. This shift in perspective can lead to profound relationships that provide both support and inspiration on their life journey.

Lastly, nurturing relationships within the community aligns seamlessly with the Life Path 5's affinity for travel and adventure. By forming connections with diverse individuals, Life Path 5s can embark on new journeys that broaden their horizons. These relationships can also serve as a source of encouragement when navigating change, providing a safety net that fosters resilience and adaptability. Ultimately, by investing time and energy into nurturing relationships, Life Path 5 individuals can create a vibrant community that supports their quest for self-discovery and personal growth.

www.ingramcontent.com/pod-product-compliance
Lightning Source LLC
Chambersburg PA
CBHW062125040426
42337CB00044B/4207